# JOKES
## for
# BOYS

JOKES FOR BOYS

Summersdale Publishers Ltd
46 West Street
Chichester
West Sussex
PO19 1RP
UK

www.summersdale.com

Printed and bound in the Czech Republic

ISBN: 978-1-84953-472-7

Substantial discounts on bulk quantities of Summersdale books are available to corporations, professional associations and other organisations. For details contact Nicky Douglas by telephone: +44 (0) 1243 756902, fax: +44 (0) 1243 786300 or email: nicky@summersdale.com.

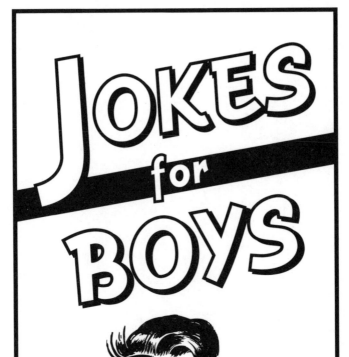

# JOKES for BOYS

Harry Hilton

summersdale

# Contents

Bat and Bawl Laughing.................................................6

What Do You Get if You Cross........................................16

The Court of Comedy..................................................23

Witty Waiter........................................................30

Farmyard Fun.........................................................34

Mathematical Mayhem..................................................40

What Do You Call.....................................................44

Creepy-Crawly Capers.................................................54

Stomach Fillers......................................................64

Sniggering Spooks....................................................73

What's The Difference Between........................................81

Monkeying Around.....................................................85

I Came, I Saw, I Laughed.............................................89

Burps, Barf and Bottom Behaviour.....................................92

Nine-to-Five Nonsense...............................................100

Coiled Up with Laughter.............................................105

Tummy-tickling Technology...........................................109

Powerful Punchlines.................................................114

Study Hard, Laugh Harder............................................118

# Bat and Bawl Laughing

How did the basketball
court get wet?

The players dribbled all over it.

How do basketball players stay cool?

They sit next to their fans.

Why did the chicken get sent off?

For persistent fowl play.

Why didn't the sandwich show
up to rugby training?

Because he was only a sub.

Why will an artist never win
a game of rugby?

Because they keep drawing.

Why was Cinderella so bad at rugby?

She kept running away from the ball.

Why couldn't the bicycle play
in the rugby match?

Because it was two-tyred.

Why is it unwise to play rugby on safari?

Because there are too many cheetahs.

Why did the boy hit his test
paper with a tennis racket?

He wanted to ace the exam.

What do you get if you cross a skunk
and a pair of tennis rackets?

Ping-pong.

Why did Robin get sent off the field?

Because he broke his bat, man.

Two cricket teammates were having a pint.
One said to the other, 'What's up? You're
looking miserable.' The other replied, 'I am.
My doctor told me I can't play cricket.' His
friend looked surprised and said, 'I didn't
know he was at the game on Sunday.'

What did the cricketer say when
the journalist asked him to explain
his poor batting average?

I'm stumped.

Why is it called a hat-trick?

Because it's performed by a bowler.

Doctor, doctor, I feel like a cricket ball.

You'll soon be over that.

Doctor, doctor, every time I use my cricket bat I feel like crying.

Perhaps it's a weeping willow.

After a bad day's play, the cricketer who had dropped six catches was getting dressed in the changing rooms. Sniffling, he said, 'I think I've caught a cold.' His captain, who was changing nearby replied, 'Thank goodness you can catch something.'

What part of a football pitch smells nicest?

The scenter spot.

How did the football pitch
end up as a triangle?

Somebody took a corner.

James was late for school. When his teacher asked him why, James replied, 'Sorry, Miss, I was dreaming about a football match.' She looked confused and said, 'But that still doesn't explain why you're late.' He replied, 'There was extra time.'

Why don't grasshoppers go to
many football matches?

They prefer cricket matches.

What do you get if you cross a football team with a bunch of crazy jokers?

Mad-jester United.

What's black and white and black and white and black and white?

A Newcastle fan rolling down a hill.

What's red, white and smiling?

The Sunderland fan who pushed him.

What's a Birmingham City fan's least favourite ice cream flavour?

Aston Vanilla.

What do you get if you cross a
footballer with a mythical creature?

A centaur forward.

Why do magicians make great footballers?

Because they do hat-tricks.

Why don't they build football
stadiums on the moon?

Because there's no atmosphere.

Why should you never invite a football
player to your dinner party?

Because he would spend the
whole time dribbling.

Why did the golfer always wear
two pairs of trousers?

In case he got a hole in one.

Doctor, doctor, I think I'm a golf ball.

Well, you've come a fair way to see me.

What's the difference between a grumpy
golfer and a cheerful golfer?

Roughly twenty-five strokes.

Golfer: I would move the whole of heaven and
the entire earth to break par on this hole.

Caddie: I'd recommend heaven, sir. You
couldn't move any more earth if you tried.

Golfer: How do you think I
could improve my game?

Caddie: Have a break from it
for a couple of weeks, sir.

Golfer: Good idea. Then what?

Caddie: Take up cricket.

Two worms lived in the rough on the
seventh hole.

First worm: There's a man swinging
a club around above us – I think
he's going to squash us!

Second worm: Hop onto that round white
thing, it's the only thing he hasn't hit yet.

Why is a poor golfer like an old car?

They both go 'putt, putt, putt'.

What do you get if you cross a frog with a rabbit?

A bunny ribbit.

What do you get if you cross
a duck with a firework?

A firequacker.

What do you get if you cross a
snake with shortcrust pastry?

A pie-thon.

What do you get if you cross
a Mars bar with an elk?

Chocolate moose.

What do you get if you cross
a parrot with a centipede?

A walkie-talkie.

What do you get if you cross a
cow, a sheep and a goat?

The Milkybaa kid.

What do you get if you cross a
duck with a steamroller?

A flat duck.

What do you get if you cross a
baby deer with a hornet?

Bambee.

What do you get if you cross a
hedgehog with a boa constrictor?

A few feet of barbed wire.

What do you get if you cross
fishing with a rabbit?

A hare net.

What do you get if you cross a
glow-worm with some beer?

Light ale.

What do you get if you cross a
doorbell with a hummingbird?

A humdinger.

What do you get if you cross a
cow with an out of date map?

Udderly lost.

What do you get if you cross
a parrot with a shark?

A bird that will talk your ear off.

What do you get if you cross
a canary with a mole?

A miner bird.

What do you get if you cross
an artist with a policeman?

A brush with the law.

What do you get if you cross
some ants with some ticks?

All sorts of antics.

What do you get if you cross
a sheep with a kangaroo?

A woolly jumper.

What do you get if you cross a
parrot with a woodpecker?

A bird that talks in Morse code.

What do you get if you cross
a cactus with a pig?

A porkerpine.

What do you get if you cross a
policeman with a telegram?

Copper wire.

What do you get if you cross
a zebra with a kangaroo?

A stripy jumper.

What do you get if you cross
a pig with an Eskimo?

A polar boar.

# The Court of Comedy

A policeman was called out to a fancy dress party by disgruntled neighbours. He arrested a man dressed as a robber, who later turned out to be a High Court judge. Well you know what they say: you should never book a judge by his cover.

A man was in a hurry to get his son to a doctor's appointment on time. After taking a wrong turn he made an illegal U-turn. 'Whoops!' he said to his son, 'I don't think I should've made that turn.' His son looked out of the back window and said, 'I think it's OK, Dad, the police car driving behind us just did the same thing.'

A policeman was out on patrol when he saw a woman knitting while driving. 'Pull over!' he shouted out of his car window. 'No officer,' she replied. 'It's a hat!'

Policeman: I'm going to have to ask you to put your dog on a lead – it was chasing that man on a bicycle.

Dog walker: That's ridiculous, Rex can't even ride a bike.

Two men were robbing a block of flats when they heard sirens approaching. The first man said, 'I can hear the cops coming – jump!' His thieving buddy screeched, 'But we're on the thirteenth floor!' The first man grabbed his partner and replied, 'Get a grip – this is no time to be superstitious!'

A shipment of expensive soaps were stolen from the dockyard.

Police say the thieves made a clean getaway.

A policeman pulled over someone driving erratically and was surprised when the man fell out of the car. 'You're drunk!' he declared, shocked by the man's state. 'Thank goodness for that,' slurred the driver. 'I thought the steering had gone!'

Policeman: I'm afraid I'll have to
lock you up for the night.

Man: Oh really? What's the charge?

Policeman: Oh, there's no charge.
It's all part of the service.

Did you hear about the police station
that had its toilets stolen?

The coppers had nothing to go on.

Did you hear about the woman
whose wig was stolen?

The police are combing the area.

What's the difference between a dead lawyer
on the road and a dead cat on the road?

There are skid marks in front of the cat.

Why are lawyers buried 18 feet under
rather than just 6 feet under?

Because deep, deep down they're good people.

What do you call a clairvoyant dwarf
who's on the run from the police?

A small medium at large.

What did the robber say to the lady
who caught him stealing her silver?

I'm at your service, madam.

What do you get when you
pour cement on a burglar?

A hardened criminal.

Why did the burglar cut the legs off his bed?

He wanted to lie low for a while.

A flustered bank robber ran into a bank, pointed a banana at one of the cashiers and shouted, 'This is a muck-up!' 'Don't you mean a stick-up?' asked the cashier. 'No,' said the robber, 'it's definitely a muck-up. I forgot my gun!'

A policeman was escorting a man he'd arrested to the station when his hat fell off and rolled away. 'Would you like me to get that for you?' asked the considerate arrestee. 'I wasn't born yesterday,' said the officer. 'You stay here and I'll get it.'

Why was the fountain pen sent to prison?

To do a long sentence.

What type of burglary is not dangerous?

A safe robbery.

What did the burglar say to the
watchmaker as he stole from his shop?

Sorry to take so much of your valuable time.

Who is the biggest gangster in the ocean?

Al Caprawn.

# WITTY WAITER

Waiter, this soup tastes funny.

Why aren't you laughing, then?

Waiter, your thumb is in my soup!

Don't worry, it's not hot.

Waiter, there is a caterpillar on my dessert!

Don't worry, sir, there's no extra charge.

Waiter, there is a fly in my soup!

Don't worry, sir, that spider on your
bread roll will soon get him.

Waiter, this coffee is disgusting,
it tastes like earth!

Yes, sir, it was ground yesterday.

Waiter, is there soup on the menu?

Not any more, madam, I wiped it off.

Waiter, this boiled egg is bad!

Don't blame me, sir, I only laid the table.

Waiter, there is a flea in my soup!

Well, tell him to hop it.

Waiter, there is a fly in my soup!

Yes, sir, he committed insecticide this morning.

Waiter, there is a snail in my salad!

I'm sorry, madam, I didn't realise
you were vegetarian.

Waiter, there is a maggot
swimming in my soup!

Don't worry, sir, he won't last long in there.

Waiter, there is a slug in my roast dinner!

Didn't you see the sign, madam
– no pets allowed.

# FARMYARD FUN

Why did the ram fall
over the cliff?

Because he didn't see
the ewe turn.

What is a horse's favourite sport?

Stable tennis.

What is the easiest way to
count a herd of cattle?

With a cowculator.

What did the baby chick say when he
saw his mother sitting on an orange?

Dad, look what Mama laid.

What do you call a pig
running around naked?

Streaky bacon.

What is the slowest horse in the world?

A clothes horse.

Why do pigs never recover from illness?

Because you have to kill them
before you cure them.

What do you call a pig who's been
arrested for dangerous driving?

A road hog.

What do you call sheep that
live in the same barn?

Pen friends.

How do chickens dance?

Chick to chick.

Which dance will a chicken not do?

The foxtrot.

What do you call a bull who tells jokes?

Laugh-a-bull.

What do chicken families do
on Saturday afternoons?

They go on peck-nics.

Why did the chick disappoint his mother?

He wasn't what he was cracked up to be.

Is chicken soup good for your soul?

Not if you're the chicken.

Which day of the week do
chickens hate most?

Fry-day.

What kind of tie does a pig wear?

A pig's tie.

What is the opposite of cock-a-doodle-doo?

Cock-a-doodle-don't.

Why was the lamb told off?

He didn't say 'thank ewe'.

How do pigs travel to hospital?

In a hambulance.

What did the horse say when he fell?

Help, I've fallen and I can't giddyup.

Why do milking stools only have three legs?

Because the cow's got the udder.

# MATHEMATICAL MAYHEM

Teacher: If I had eight apples in my right hand and ten apples in my left hand, what would I have?

Student: Huge hands, sir.

A rubber band pistol was confiscated
from algebra class because it was
a weapon of maths disruption.

I used to hate maths but then I
realised decimals have a point.

Teacher: If eggs were fifty pence a dozen,
how many would you get for forty pence?

Pupil: None.

Teacher: None?

Pupil: If I had forty pence, I'd
buy a bag of crisps.

Why did the boy eat his maths homework?

Because the teacher told him
it was a piece of cake.

Why was the maths book sad?

Because it had too many problems.

Why didn't the two fours want any dinner?

Because they already eight!

Pupil: Miss, I think number
six is scared of seven.

Teacher: Why is that?

Pupil: Because seven eight nine.

Pupil: Sir, my dog ate my homework.

Teacher: And where's your dog now?

Pupil: He's at the vet's – he
doesn't like maths either.

Why couldn't the student divide by two?

She didn't know the half of it.

Teacher: How many seconds
are there in a year?

Pupil: Twelve! January the
2nd, February the 2nd...

Teacher: Whenever I ask you a
question, I want you to answer
altogether. What is nine times four?

Class: Altogether!

Why do plants hate maths?

Because it gives them square roots.

# WHAT DO YOU CALL...

What do you call a
bee born in May?

A maybe.

What do you call a lion that has eaten your mother's sister?

An aunt-eater.

What do you call a flock of birds that fly in formation?

The red sparrows.

What do you call a one-legged lady?

Eileen.

What do you call a bee that never stops complaining?

A grumble bee.

What do you call a fish with no eyes?

A fsh.

What do you call a fish with three eyes?

A fiiish.

What do you call a deer with no eyes?

No idea.

What do you call an elephant that
has had too much to drink?

Trunk.

What do you call a big fish that makes you an offer you can't refuse?

The Codfather.

What do you call a parrot taking a shower?

Polly saturated.

What do you call an overweight ghost that haunts an opera house?

The fat tum of the opera.

What do you call a donkey with three legs?

A wonkey.

What do you call someone who
makes tiny models of fish?

A scale modeller.

What do you call a dentist in the army?

A drill sergeant.

What do you call someone
who dances on old cars?

A Morris dancer.

What do you call a show full of lions?

The mane event.

What do you call a rabbit sitting in a trifle?

A cream bunny.

What do you call a sheep with no legs?

A cloud.

What do you call a dog that is
always getting into fights?

A boxer.

What do you call the country's best dad?

Top of the pops.

What do you call a film about ducklings?

A duckumentary.

What do you call a very rude bird?

A mockingbird.

What do you call a chocolatey snack that pokes fun at tunnelling mammals?

A mole-teaser.

What do you call a policeman with blonde hair?

A fair cop.

What do you call a Scottish parrot?

A macaw.

What do you call a fish riding a motorcycle?

A motor pike.

What do you call a traffic warden
who never hands out fines?

A terrific warden.

What do you call an amazing
artwork created by a rodent?

A mouseterpiece.

What do you call parrot food?

Polly filla.

What do you call a cat with eight
legs that likes to swim?

An octopuss.

What do you call a clever duck?

A wise quacker.

What do you call a crazy chicken?

A cuckoo cluck.

What do you call a man with
a spade on his head?

Doug.

What do you call a man who's
lost the spade from his head?

Douglas.

What do you call a man with no shins?

Tony.

What do you call an Italian with a rubber toe?

Roberto.

# CREEPY-CRAWLY CAPERS

Why was the fly dancing on
the top of the lemonade bottle?

Because the label said
'Twist to open'.

What flies around your light at night
and can bite off your head?

A tiger moth.

What games do ants play with elephants?

Squash.

Why are ant colonies free from disease?

Because they are full of antibodies.

What kind of ant is good at maths?

An accountant.

How many ants are needed
to fill an apartment?

Ten ants.

Which pillar doesn't need holding up?

A caterpillar.

What does a caterpillar do
on New Year's Day?

Turns over a new leaf.

What goes 99... clonk, 99... clonk, 99... clonk?

A centipede with a wooden leg.

Why was the centipede dropped
from the insect football team?

He took too long to put his boots on.

What is worse than a shark with toothache?

A centipede with athlete's foot.

What has fifty legs but can't walk?

Half a centipede.

What did the boy centipede
say to the girl centipede?

You've got a lovely pair of legs,
you've got a lovely pair of legs,
you've got a lovely pair of legs...

What kind of wig can hear?

An earwig.

What did the earwig say as
it fell down the stairs?

Ear we go.

What did the clean dog say to the flea?

Long time no flea.

What is a flea's favourite book?

The Itch-hiker's Guide to the Galaxy.

Why were the flies playing
football in a saucer?

They were playing for the cup.

What did the firefly say as he was leaving?

Got to glow now.

What is green and can jump
a mile in a minute?

A grasshopper with hiccups.

What has antlers and sucks blood?

A moose-quito.

What do insects learn at school?

Mothmatics.

What is a myth?

A female moth.

Why did the moth nibble a hole in the carpet?

He wanted to see the floor show.

What's the biggest moth that's ever lived?

A mammoth.

What happened when the spider got angry?

He went up the wall.

How do you know your kitchen floor is dirty?

The slugs leave a trail on the
floor that reads 'clean me'.

What was the snail doing on the motorway?

About one mile a day.

How do snails get their shells so shiny?

They use snail varnish.

What do you do when two
snails have a fight?

Leave them to slug it out.

What did the maggot say to his friend
when he got stuck in an apple?

Worm your way out of that one.

How can you tell which end
of a worm is which?

Tickle it in the middle and
see which end laughs.

Why was the glow-worm unhappy?

Because her children weren't that bright.

**What did one maggot say to another?**

What's a nice maggot like you
doing in a joint like this?

**What did the woodworm say to the chair?**

It's been nice gnawing you.

**Why are glow-worms good
to carry in your bag?**

They can lighten your load.

Two ants were sprinting across the top
of a cereal box. One screamed to the
other, 'Why are we running so fast?'
The other one shouted back, 'Because
it says "tear along the dotted line"!'

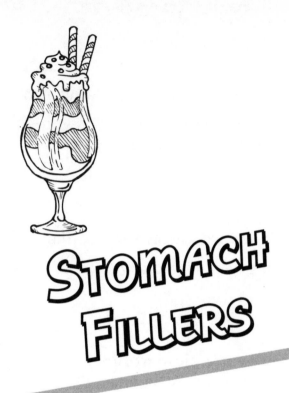

# STOMACH FILLERS

What did the spectator say
when the cake sprinted past?

Scone.

Why did the ice scream?

Because he heard the lolly pop.

A dairy factory worker lost her
job when she fell in a vat.

She was sacked for getting in the whey.

What flies and wobbles?

A jellycopter.

Why do the French love eating snails?

Because they can't stand fast food.

Why don't gingerbread men wear shorts?

Because their legs are crumby.

Why are prunes worth buying?

You get a good run for your money.

How did the man drown in the fruit cake?

He was pulled under by a strong currant.

Why couldn't the sesame seed
leave the blackjack table?

He was on a roll.

What should you feed a hungry computer?

Chips. One byte at a time.

Why did the bread rush down the hill?

Because he saw the cheese roll.

What inspired the salad to take up cooking?

Watching the pasta bake.

What happened to the jug of
milk in the punch-up?

He got creamed.

What do cannibals order when
they have a takeaway?

Pizza with everyone on it.

What do astronauts put in their sandwiches?

Launching meat.

Why couldn't the burger stop smiling?

He was in a Happy Meal.

Why did the French fries turn the music up?

To see the milk shake.

Why is a sofa like a roast chicken?

Because they're both full of stuffing.

What's yellow and dangerous?

Shark-infested custard.

What do cats call mice on skateboards?

Meals on wheels.

Sister: Why do you eat so fast?

Brother: I want to eat as much as possible before losing my appetite.

What did the mayonnaise say
to the refrigerator?

Close the door, I'm dressing!

Brother: Would you like some Egyptian pie?

Sister: What's Egyptian pie?

Brother: You know, the kind
Mummy used to make.

Why did the man eat at the bank?

He wanted to eat rich food.

What's the worst thing about
being an octopus?

Washing your hands before dinner.

Why did the man stare at the
can of orange juice?

Because it said 'concentrate.'

How does the man on the moon eat his food?

In satellite dishes.

Where do boxers cry?

In an onion ring.

71

Why did the man climb onto the
roof of the fast food restaurant?

They told him the meal was on the house.

Would octopus make good fast food?

You must be squidding.

Where do burgers like to dance?

At a meat ball.

What did the hamburger say to the pickle?

You're dill-icious.

# Sniggering Spooks

Why did the skeleton go
to the party alone?

He had no body to go with him.

What is a skeleton's favourite food?

Spare ribs.

Did you hear about the guy who had his left ear bitten off by a werewolf?

He's all right now.

What kind of music do mummies listen to?

Wrap music.

What is a vampire's favourite fruit?

Necktarine.

What do you call a vampire
who does gymnastics?

An acrobat.

A skeleton walks into a bar and
says, 'I'll have a beer and a mop.'

Why does Dracula have no friends?

Because he's a pain in the neck.

What do vampires have at
eleven o'clock every day?

A coffin break.

Where do vampires go on holiday?
The Isle of Fright.

Why did the ghost go to hospital?
He wanted his ghoul stones removed.

What do you get if you cross
Dracula with Al Capone?
A fangster.

Where do Chinese vampires come from?
Fanghai.

How does Frankenstein's
monster sit in his chair?

Bolt upright.

What did the zombie's friend say when
he introduced him to his girlfriend?

Good grief! Where did you dig her up from?

What did the monster say to his psychiatrist?

I feel abominable.

What do you call a monster
with a wooden head?

Edward.

What's a monster's favourite play?

Romeo and Ghouliet.

Why did the monster eat a light bulb?

Because he was in need of a light snack.

Why wasn't there any food left
after the monster party?

Because everyone was a goblin.

What does a ghost wear when it's raining?

Boooooooooooooooooots.

What is a ghost's favourite road?

Dead End.

What is a ghost's favourite rock?

Tombstone.

Where is a zombie's favourite place to swim?

The Dead Sea.

How did the zombie feel after
a long day at work?

Dead tired.

Why was the baby ghost crying?

He had a boo-boo.

What horses go out after dusk?

Nightmares.

What's the difference between
a fish and a piano?

You can't tuna fish.

What's the difference between
a mosquito and a fly?

Try zipping up a mosquito.

What's the difference between an
inflatable dartboard and a kilo of lard?

One is a fat lot of good and the
other is a good lot of fat.

What's the difference between an injured
lion and an English summer's day?

One roars with pain and the
other pours with rain.

What's the difference between a well-
dressed man and a tired dog?

One wears a suit and tie, the other just pants.

What's the difference between a school day and a ball of string?

The string won't go on for ever.

What's the difference between a boxer and a man with a cold?

One knows his blows and the other blows his nose.

What's the difference between a flea and a wolf?

One prowls on the hairy and the other howls on the prairie.

What's the difference between chopped beef and pea soup?

Everyone can chop beef, but not everyone can pea soup.

What's the difference between a
saloon and an elephant fart?

One's a bar room and the
other is a BAROOOOM!

What's the difference between
a violinist and a dog?

The dog knows when to stop scratching.

# Monkeying Around

Why was the monkey lonely?

Because the banana split.

Why do gorillas have big nostrils?

Where else are they going to
put those big fingers?

Why did the orang-utan get
told off at school?

He was monkeying around.

What did the monkey say when he
accidentally cut his tail in half?

It won't be long now.

What key opens a banana?

A monkey.

Why did the monkey like the banana?

Because it had appeal.

Why was the monkey scared
to go to the barbeque?

Because she thought they might gorilla.

Why did the monkey get lost in the forest?

Because jungle is massive.

What do you call a monkey
at the top of the tree?

A branch manager.

Where do monkeys hear rumours?

On the apevine.

What do you do with a blue monkey?

Cheer it up.

Why did the chimpanzee cross the road?

Because he had to take care of
some monkey business.

# I Came, I Saw, I Laughed

My girlfriend has just left me, saying I spend too much time devoted to my studies of Roman numerals. I'm L I V I D.

Why were the early days of
history called the Dark Ages?

Because there were so many knights.

Why is England the wettest country?

Because the queen has
reigned there for years.

How did the Vikings send secret messages?

By Norse code.

Who invented fractions?

Henry the 1/5th.

Who made King Arthur's round table?

Sir–Cumference

How was the Roman Empire cut in half?

With a pair of Caesars.

Teacher: What did Henry VIII do
when he came to the throne?

Pupil: He sat on it.

My father is so old that when he was in
school, history was called current affairs.

# BURPS, BARF AND BOTTOM BEHAVIOUR

What's brown and
sits in the forest?

Winnie's poo.

Two brothers are getting ready for school. One boy is in the kitchen, having a bowl of cornflakes, while the other is frantically looking for his show-and-tell collection. 'I'm sure I put it in here somewhere,' he says, before remembering he'd left it in the kitchen. Looking on the table he notices his brother's bowl of cereal. 'Oh, so you found my scab collection then.'

There were two flies on the toilet.

One flew away, but the other got peed off.

Did you know diarrhoea is hereditary?

Yes – it runs in your jeans.

Did you hear about the blind skunk?

He's dating a fart.

A shopkeeper greets a customer, who asks him where the toilet rolls are. 'Here you go,' says the shopkeeper. 'Did you want blue, peach, primrose yellow...?' 'White will do,' replies the man. 'I prefer to colour it myself.'

While waiting at the doctor's surgery, a man lets rip a really loud fart. Trying to look nonchalant he turns to the woman next to him as if nothing has happened. 'Do you have a copy of today's paper I could borrow?' he asks. 'No,' she replies, 'but if you put your hand out of the window you can rip some leaves off that bush.'

What's brown and sticky?

A brown stick.

At church a little girl tells her mother she's going to be sick. Her mother tells her to do it in the bushes round the back of the church. The girl leaves and comes back after about five minutes. Her mother asks her if she threw up. 'Yes,' the girl says. 'But I didn't have to go round the back, there was a little box by the front door that said, "For the Sick".'

Did you hear about the constipated mathematician?

He worked it out with a pencil.

Two flies were sitting on a dog poo. One farted and the other one turned to him and snapped, 'Do you mind? Can't you see I'm eating?'

What's the definition of bravery?

A man with diarrhoea risking a fart.

There are three ladies in a waiting room. The first lady compliments the second on her perfume and asks her what it is. 'A special blend, only available in France,' she replies haughtily. The first lady then announces that her perfume is unique, created just for her in a perfumery in Egypt. They look expectantly at the third, waiting for her contribution. She stands up and lets out a very stinky fart. 'Cauliflower curry,' she says proudly, 'from the Indian down the road.'

Doctor, doctor, I've got wind! Can you give me something?

Yes – here's a kite.

Why did the baker have brown hands?

Because he kneaded a poo.

A woman goes to see the doctor because she can't stop farting. 'It's not a huge problem because they don't smell or make a noise, but I just want them to stop. Even though you haven't noticed, I have already farted a few times in this office. Can you prescribe me something?' Looking pained, the doctor begins writing out a prescription. 'I'm prescribing some decongestants for your nose,' he says, 'and referring you for a hearing test.'

Why do people whistle when they're sitting on the toilet?

Because it helps them remember which end they need to wipe.

An old couple are lying in bed when the man does a big, noisy fart. 'One nil!' he exclaims gleefully. In response, the old lady rolls over and does a huge fart in his direction. 'One all!' she shouts. This carries on until the score is three apiece. It is then the old man's turn again but try as he might, he cannot fart. He tries so hard that he ends up pooing in the bed. Before his wife notices he shouts, 'Half time! Switch sides!'

What do you call someone who doesn't fart in public?
A private tutor.

Two puddles of sick went out for a stroll. One of them sighed. The other asked, 'What is it?' The first replied, 'Only nostalgia. You see, I was brought up around here.'

A woman walks into a very expensive shoe shop to admire the display. Leaning over to pick up a particularly beautiful pair of high-heeled shoes, she accidentally lets out a fart. Seeing no one around, she thinks she has got away with it. Just then a salesman walks up to her and asks if she would like any assistance. She asks about the price of the beautiful shoes. 'Well, madam,' he replies, 'if just touching them makes you fart, you are going to poo your pants when you find out how much they cost.'

Why did the grumpy old man take toilet paper to the party with him?

Because he was a party pooper.

# NINE-TO-FIVE NONSENSE

Why did all the staff at the paper company lose their jobs?

Because the company folded.

A new employee was heading home late when he spotted the manager in the photocopy room holding a piece of paper next to the shredder. The manager looked confused so, seeing his chance to win favour, the new employee offered to help. 'This is a very important document,' said the manager. 'My secretary's left for the night, and I can't get this thing to work.' 'No problem,' said the young worker. He took the piece of paper, turned on the shredder and inserted the document. 'You got it working! Fantastic!' said the manager excitedly. 'Now can I have three copies?'

Which sea creature's job is it to keep the ocean clean?

A mermaid.

Salesman: This computer will cut
your workload by 50 per cent.

Office Manager: That's great!
I'll take two of them.

What did the electrician say when his
son didn't come home on time?

Wire you insulate?

A new client had just come in to see a
famous lawyer. 'Can you tell me how
much you charge?' said the client. 'Of
course,' the lawyer replied, 'I charge £200
to answer three questions!' 'Well that's
a bit steep, isn't it?' 'Yes it is,' said the
lawyer, 'and what's your third question?'

Doctor: Did you take the
patient's temperature?

Nurse: No. Is it missing?

Doctor: Nurse, how is that little boy
doing, the one who swallowed money?

Nurse: No change yet.

Did you hear about the blind carpenter
who picked up his hammer and saw?

If you're an optimist, the glass is half full.

If you're a pessimist, the glass is half empty.

And if you're an engineer, the glass is
two times bigger than it needs to be.

There was a nasty smell in the office, so one girl said, 'Please will someone do something about their deodorant – it obviously isn't working.' The bloke sitting next to her swung round and announced, 'Well, it can't be mine because I'm not wearing any.'

A painter was hired to paint a row of houses. On the first day he painted five houses, on the second he coated two houses, and on the third day he only managed half a house. His boss took him aside and asked, 'Why are you doing less work each day?' The worker replied, 'Because every day I am getting further away from the paint can.'

# COILED UP WITH LAUGHTER

Why wouldn't the lizard go
on the weighing machine?

Because he had his own scales.

What subject do snakes love at school?

Hissssstory.

Why are snakes hard to fool?

They have no legs to pull.

What do snake couples have
on their bath towels?

Hiss and Hers.

What did the python say to the viper?

I've got a crush on you.

What's the best thing about deadly snakes?

They've got poisonality.

Why did the python do national service?

He was coiled up.

Why did the viper viper nose?

Because the adder adder handkerchief.

What do you give a sick snake?

Asp-rin.

What do baby pythons play with?

Rattlesnakes.

What's long, green and goes hith?

A snake with a lisp.

Which snakes are found on cars?

Windscreen vipers.

What kind of tiles can't you stick on walls?

Reptiles.

# Tummy-TICKLING TECHNOLOGY

How can you tell if a
bee is on the phone?

You get a buzzy signal.

Why didn't the mouse cross the road?

Its cord wasn't long enough.

What did one keyboard say
to the other keyboard?

Sorry, you're not my type.

What is an astronaut's favourite
key on a computer keyboard?

The space bar.

Why did the student kick the
classroom computer?

Someone told him he was supposed
to boot up the system.

Customer: I think I've got a
bug in my computer.

Repairman: Does your computer
make a humming noise?

Customer: Yes.

Repairman: Then it must be a humbug!

What video game character do
you call if you're moving?

Pacman.

A farmer had trouble counting his crop
so he got a computer. One day he was
going to his computer when he slipped
on some hay and his head became stuck
in the computer. His son called 999 and
said, 'There's a farmer in the Dell!'

Where do computers go to dance?

The disk-o.

Why did the tree get a computer?

To log in.

Why did the TV cross the road?

Because it wanted to be a flat screen.

What do you get if you cross a
football player with a payphone?

A wide receiver.

What did the spider do on the computer?

It made a website.

What did the computer do at lunchtime?

It had a byte to eat.

What does a baby computer call his father?

Data.

Why did the computer keep sneezing?

It had a virus.

Why was the computer so
tired when it got home?

Because it had a hard drive.

# POWERFUL PUNCHLINES

What is a pig's favourite
karate move?

The pork chop.

He's an ambidextrous fighter. He can get knocked out with either hand.

What does a boxer ask for at the hairdresser's?

An uppercut.

During a practical exercise at a military police base, the instructor was giving the class instruction in unarmed self-defence. After he presented a number of different situations in which they might find themselves, he asked a student, 'What steps would you take if someone were coming at you with a large, sharp knife?' The student replied, 'BIG ones.'

The best way to learn judo is to walk through a spider's web.

What do you do to a wrestler at night?

Put him in a sleeper hold.

A fighter was taking a beating. When the bell rang, he staggered to his corner. Dousing him with a bucket of water, his manager suggested, 'Let him hit you with the left for a change. Your face is crooked!'

Why did the karate comedian get demoted?

The punchline was weak.

My cousin was an incredibly tough
man. He was a karate black belt who
eventually joined the army. Every
time he saluted he hurt himself.

What do you serve at a kick-boxing party?

Punch.

# Study Hard, Laugh Harder

Teacher: This is the fifth day this week you've had to stay after school. What do you have to say for yourself?

Pupil: I'm certainly glad it's Friday.

Teacher: Why are you late?

Pupil: Because of the sign.

Teacher: What sign?

Pupil: The one that says,
'School ahead, go slow.'

Father: Son, come here! What's all this
about? Your teacher says he finds it
impossible to teach you anything.

Son: I told you he was no good.

Pupil: Sir, would you punish me
for something I didn't do?

Teacher: Of course not.

Pupil: Good, because I didn't
do my homework.

Son: Dad, I'm tired of doing homework.

Father: Now, son, hard work
never killed anyone.

Son: I know, but I don't want to be the first.

If teachers are so smart, how come their
book is the only one with the answers in it?

Why was the head teacher worried?

Because there were so many
rulers in the school.

Ninety two per cent of cross-eyed teachers
have difficulty controlling their pupils.

How do you get straight As?

By using a ruler.

Why did the kid study in the airplane?

Because he wanted a higher education.

What did the pencil sharpener
say to the pencil?

Stop going in circles and get to the point.

Dad: What did you learn in school today?

Son: Not enough, I have to go back tomorrow.

Why did the teacher wear
sunglasses to work?

Because his class was so bright.

After noticing a child in class pulling
faces, a primary schoolteacher took the
troublemaker aside and said, 'When I was
little my mummy told me if I pulled faces the
wind would change and it would get stuck
that way.' The naughty boy replied, 'Well,
miss, you can't say you weren't warned.'

What do opticians and teachers
have in common?

They both test pupils.

Why isn't whispering permitted in class?

Because it's not aloud.

Teacher: You will be allowed thirty
minutes for each question.

Pupil: How long do we get
to write the answers?

Why did the student say his
marks were 'underwater'?

Because they were all below Cs.

Why did the student write
on his toes in class?

He was trying to think on his feet.

Why did the schoolboy wear stilts?

Because he went to a high school.

A teacher was taking his first class at a
new school. After introducing himself he
announced, 'Stand up if you think you're
stupid.' Nobody moved, and then after a
minute, one pupil stood up. 'So you think
you're an idiot, then?' said the teacher.
'No,' replied the pupil, 'I just didn't want
you standing up all on your own.'

What kind of exams do horses take?

Hay Levels.

A boy came home from school and told his mother he couldn't do science any more. 'Why not?' asked his mother. 'Because I blew something up,' explained her son. 'What?' she said. 'The school,' he replied.

Mother: Why was your exam score so low last week?

Son: Absence.

Mother: What, you missed the exam?

Son: No, but the girl who sits next to me did.

Why couldn't one maths book
help the other maths book?

Because it had its own problems.

Why did the little boy eat two pound coins?

Because his mother told him
it was his lunch money.

# Acknowledgements

Thanks to Summersdale's Facebook and Twitter friends who sent in their jokes to be included in the book. They are:

Gillian Petley-Jones
Val Rayner
Rodger Kibble
Christopher Dingle
Nicolas Jared
David Rayner
Samantha Kluttz

If you're interested in finding out more about our books, find us on Facebook at Summersdale Publishers and follow us on Twitter at @Summersdale.

# www.summersdale.com